DRABNE OF DOLE

MONSTERS OF MYTHOLOGY

25 VOLUMES

MONSTERS OF MYTHOLOGY

DRABNE OF DOLE

Bernard Evslin

CHELSEA HOUSE PUBLISHERS

New York   Philadelphia

1990

EDITOR
Remmel Nunn

ART DIRECTOR
Maria Epes

PICTURE RESEARCHER
Susan Quist

SENIOR DESIGNER
Marjorie Zaum

EDITORIAL ASSISTANTS
Seeta Chaganti, Nate Eaton, Mark Rifkin

First Printing

1   3   5   7   9   8   6   4   2

Library of Congress Cataloging-in-Publication Data

Evslin, Bernard.
Drabne of Dole/Bernard Evslin.

p.   cm.—(Monsters of mythology.)
Summary: The Celtic hero Finn McCool outwits the sorceress Drabne
of Dole, acquiring the magical knowledge he needs to avenge the
death of his father Cuhal.
ISBN 1-55546-245-6
1. Mythology, Celtic—Juvenile literature.
[1. Finn MacCool. 2. Mythology, Celtic] I. Title.
II. Series: Evslin, Bernard.
Monsters of mythology.
BL900.E87   1990   398.22'09415—dc20
89-25358   CIP   AC

Printed in Singapore

To STEVE CLINTON, who guards a treasure

Characters

Monsters

Drabne of Dole	A fearsome shape-changing sorceress; the Fish Hag and the Winter Witch (also called She of the Burning) are two of her favorite guises
Vilemurk	First among the Foul-weather Fiends
Mist Crones	Daughters of Drabne who serve Vilemurk

Gods

Amara	Goddess of the Harvest

Mortals

Finn McCool	A young hero
Murtha	His cousin and first love
Finn's Mother	A giantess; Cuhal's widow
Goll McMorna	Powerful war chief; Finn's enemy
Assorted Druids	Oak priests, reputed to be wise

Animals

Salmon of Knowledge	A unique fish, very wise, very magical
Cat	Drabne's black tom who switches sides
Falcon	Great gray hawk who quits Goll to serve Finn
Snakes	Two huge serpents, one good, one bad

Others

Thrig of Tone	Not god, demon, or mortal, but a talented elf
Master of Winds	Storm demon employed by Vilemurk

Things

Needles, pins	Belonging to Drabne's workbasket; given brief spiteful life
Scissors-bird	Most terrible denizen of workbasket. A flying shears, animated by Drabne
Harp of Dagda	Story harp of the ancient wizard bard, newly played by Finn

BOOKS BY BERNARD EVSLIN

Merchants of Venus
Heroes, Gods and Monsters of the Greek Myths
Greeks Bearing Gifts: The Epics of Achilles and Ulysses
The Dolphin Rider
Gods, Demigods and Demons
The Green Hero
Heraclea
Signs & Wonders: Tales of the Old Testament

Contents

1

A Thrig, a Witch, and Two Snakes

inn McCool was a giant but much too small for the work; the runt of the litter he was, yards shorter than his brothers or sisters, which was embarrassing. In fact, it is a better thing altogether to be a large dwarf than a small giant. Such a thing has been known to spoil someone's disposition entirely. But it didn't spoil Finn's. He quickly learned how things were in the world, and said to himself: "Can't afford to be bad tempered; not till I get a reputation."

To go back a bit, though. When Finn was an infant he shared his crib with a girl baby named Murtha, whose own mother, a giantess, had been killed by an avalanche she started herself by throwing her husband headfirst off a mountain because he'd said something rude. So Finn shared his crib with young Murtha, and his porridge bowl and his rattle and such.

Now it is well known that infants are nasty, squalling, damp objects—except to their mothers, perhaps—but this Murtha was something else. Even as an infant she was beautiful. Her skin was ivory and pink, and she was never bald for an instant, but was born with a marvelous black fleece of hair, and had eyes that were neither green nor blue, but violet—rare for eyes. And teeth—a full set of them—so that she was able to bite Finn quite early. On the other hand, her smile flashed like a stream when the sun hits it.

She was a lovely creature, and young Finn fell in love with her immediately, just like that, and had resolved to marry her before he was three days old, but decided to keep it secret awhile because he knew she wasn't ready to listen to proposals. Nevertheless, his love for her was so great that he couldn't rest for trying to win her admiration, which was difficult to do; she didn't seem to notice him particularly except when she decided to bite him or snatch his bottle. She would lie on her back dreamily watching the clouds go by—their cradle was a leather sling set in an oak tree; this is the way of giant babes—and he did not know what to do to attract her attention.

He noticed that she did not like slithery things. Worms made her unhappy. She would grab a wolfhound by the whiskers and kiss it on the nose, but spiders were a different matter entirely; she hated them and was afraid. This set Finn to thinking.

"My short time in the world has taught me that the way to a young lady's heart is by being very brave. Yes, even if you're not, you must make her believe you are; that's just as good. Now to be brave is dangerous sometimes, but if you're a lad of ideas you can get around that part maybe."

He thought and thought and put together a bit of a plan. "Now it's a fact she's afraid of worms," he said to himself. "This is quite plain. Oh yes, terrified of the tiny things, bless her heart. But why? They can't hurt her. They cannot bite or sting. Why then does she fear them? It is their shape, perhaps, for what else is there about them? And they crawl on their bellies, squiggling along, for how else do they go? Now when a worm falls off the branch into the cradle I might boldly brush it away, but that is not very impressive, after all. She might appreciate it but she would not go mad with admiration. No, no. I must do something

Even as an infant she was beautiful.

more splendid, more bold, bigger altogether. What then is a big worm? Big worm . . .

"Why, yes—a snake! That's anyone's idea of a big worm, I should think. Now if she's afraid of worms, she would go absolutely stark blue with terror, the beautiful child, if she saw a snake, a sight she has been spared so far. If only I could rescue her from a snake, ah, that would be a thing to admire. This would count as a great deed. This would win her heart. She would know her cousin Finn is a hero, and fit to be wed. There's a drawback, though. I myself am by no means partial to serpents. Why, as I lie here and think about them, I can feel myself beginning to shiver and shake. I am still but a babe, I haven't come into my strength, and I couldn't handle the loopy beast if I did meet one. Nevertheless, for all the fear and doubt, there is an idea here and I must make it grow."

So he thought and thought until his eyes grew blurred with sleep and the far star trembled and went out. When he awoke, the first tatters of mist were beginning to flush with light. He swung himself out of his bull-hide cradle, crept down the tree like a squirrel, and went into the wood. As he went he kept his eyes open and kept thinking very hard. In the deep of the wood he rested himself under a tree. A strange bird screamed. Finn shivered. It was dark in the wood, not the safe darkness of night, but a green, scary dusk of day half-hidden. The bird screamed again. In the brush something snarled and pounced. Something else spoke in pain; chipmunk perhaps, or rabbit.

"All things here eat each other," he said to himself. "The big ones eat the small ones. An uncomfortable kind of arrangement, especially if you're small."

He felt fuller of sadness than he could hold, and he wept a tear. The tear fell, but did not vanish as tears usually do. It glittered upon the leaf mold, grew brighter, rose again toward his face. It was a tiny manikin, rising out of the earth. No bigger than a twig was he, with a squinched-up little nut of a face. Upon his head glistened Finn's tear, a crystal now, milky white as the moon, lighting up a space about the little man.

"Who are you?" said Finn.

"I am the Thrig of Tone."

"*Are you* now?"

"Have you heard of me?"

"No, sir."

"An ignorant lad you are then, for I am famous."

"What for?"

"Magic mostly. Mischief some. I'm much abused in certain quarters, but I'm a good one to know, I'll tell you that. Unless I happen to take a dislike to you, in which case you will regret our acquaintance."

"I see," said Finn.

"I doubt it. The thing about me is I'm not around very often, as it happens. A powerful curse is working upon me, you see. I'm the prisoner of a spell, woven by the wickedest old witch who was ever wooed by the devil and wore a black hat to her wedding. Her name is Drabne of Dole. What can I do for you now?"

"You wish to do something for me?"

"I must."

"Why must you?"

"A condition of the curse. I'm a prisoner of the dust, you see, until the purest tear happens to fall on me. Then I come to life and wear it as a jewel and must serve the weeper, whoever it is."

"Did I weep a pure tear?"

"I'm here, am I not?"

"What makes a tear pure?"

"An extraordinary grief. Something outside the scheme of things, so odd it makes the gods laugh. And that laughter of the gods, which you know as the wind, means that someone somewhere has a grief he cannot handle. But it must be something special; plain things won't do, you know, not for the gods. They see enough of ordinary misery; they're no longer amused, they like something special. A crocodile moved to pity, perhaps; that roused me some time ago, and I had an adventure then. Or a king brought low. Yes, they like that. Or something wondrously beautiful made ugly, watching itself become so and not able to stop. All this will set the night a-howling. What they found special in you, I don't know. But here I am. And there's the wind, hear it? What *is* your problem, lad?"

No bigger than a twig was he,
with a squinched-up little nut of a face.
Upon his head glistened Finn's tear . . .

"Myself, mostly. I come of a family of giants, and am small. I love someone who does not know what love is. And I have a bold deed in mind, but am afraid. Also, something pounced and something screamed, reminding me of the world's arrangements about big things eating small ones. Well, all this made me weep, Master Thrig of Tone, sir. If you help me I shall be grateful, but I don't know how you can."

6

"What is this deed you have in mind?"

"Well, you see, sir, this young lady I admire is much upset by the sight of a worm, making me think that the sight of a snake would absolutely terrify her and make her feel very affectionate toward her rescuer."

"Think you'd be much good at fighting off serpents? They're very strong, you know, just one long muscle. Makes it awkward when you start to wrestle them. Not only that, but they've a mouthful of secret weapons. Hollow teeth that squirt poison, making even the smallest serpent deadlier than wolf or bear. You're absolutely sure it's a snake you want to choose for your first bout, young Finn?"

"I am sure."

"Well, this requires a bit of thinking. Let's see. How can we do this with the most honor to you and most effect on your little friend, and the least damage to both of you? And the most pleasure to the serpents too, for they're the kind of creature that go along with nothing unless they're pleased. Pleased, yes, that's a thought. You play a musical instrument? Flute, for instance?"

"Don't even know what that is. Sometimes, though, I shake my rattle a certain way that makes my blood dance. And Murtha sits there dancing without moving her legs."

"Rhythm section's all very well," said the thrig. "But what snakes like is melody."

He broke off a reed from a nearby clump, took out a knife no longer than a thorn and notched the reed, then gave it to Finn.

"What's this?"

"A reed, doctored according to me lights."

"What's it for?"

"Well, reeds have a hard life," said the manikin. "You must understand that in the vegetable kingdom they're nowhere. Very bottom of the list. No leaves, no scent, not even any nuisance value like weeds. They are frail stalks bowing before every wind. And yet this is their magic. Their courtesy to the wind is a very special quality. For they are the first to recognize the cruel laughter of the gods, and so are attuned to human misery. Their weakness gives strength its meaning; their lowliness makes fame shine; their pity is the best description in all the world of cruelty. The owl hitting a mouse, a wasp stinging a beetle to death, the young boy drowned in the pride of swimming, the bride realizing that she has married wrong and that her mistake has become her life—all these things that make the gods laugh and the winds howl, the reeds know first. They bow to it. And as the wind seethes through them, they rustle in a kind of music. It all becomes music in them. Music, which is the essence of all we cannot say in words. And if you take a reed and notch it in a certain way—like this—and give it to one who will whisper his own story to it, why, then a most exquisite music is made . . . ."

Finn stared at the thrig; it was hard to believe that this tiny man could produce a voice of such power.

"And now happens the greatest joke of all," continued the thrig. "A joke on the gods themselves, those jesters. For hearing the music out of the reed, why, Evil itself, or the simplified shape of evil, the snake, becomes enraptured and dances in slow loops of ecstasy. And a slight pause comes to evil arrangements. Strength is diverted from cruelty. The blackness of death is split for a moment, and a crystal light streams, making pictures in the head, and it seems to those listening that things might be different, might be better. But only for a second. Then the music stops and all goes back the way it was before. But in that moment the snake has danced and the victim forgotten fear. D'you follow me, boy?"

"Will you teach me to play this thing?"

"Let me hear you whistle this tune. I can do nothing if you have no ear."

Finn whistled. He could do that. He had amused himself in his cradle, imitating birds. The thrig nodded.

"Not entirely tone deaf, I'm glad to hear. Perhaps I can. . . . Maybe so. Very well, let us begin."

"Now?"

"Always now when it comes to learning, especially something difficult."

"But I'm hungry, I'm cold. I'm sleepy."

"Tell it to the reed."

Now it is said that the Thrig of Tone and young Finn stayed under that tree for a week of days and a week of nights piping duets. It rained sometimes and the nights were cold. Nor did they stop for food. Nixies don't eat the stuff, and the thrig had forgotten that humans do. All Finn had during this time was three mushrooms that happened to grow near where he was sitting. For thirst he drank the rain. Oh, it was a hard time he had, but it wasn't allowed to matter. The thrig was a strict teacher, and kept Finn at it. What happened then was that the lad's hunger and thirst and sleepiness and loneliness wove themselves into the music, and the reeds added their own notes of pity and joy. And at the end of their time under the oak tree you could not tell who was teacher and who was pupil; they played equally well.

They played so beautifully that the birds stopped their own singing to listen. Even the owl left off hunting, forgot her bloody hunger for a bit, and stood on a limb listening, hooting the tune softly to herself. The deer came, and wolves. Weasels, foxes, stoats, rabbits, bears, badgers, chipmunks, wild pigs. They came and stood in silent ranks at night, forgetting their enmity and fear as the moonlight sifted through the leaves and touched different fur with silver. Finally, two huge snakes came slithering out of their fearful nest and sat among their coils, weaving a slow dance.

"Enough!" cried the Thrig of Tone. "Lesson's over, young Finn. You've learned what I can teach. You can pipe and the devil can dance."

"Thank you, sir," said Finn.

"I have done my good deed without interruption, and am free at last, I hope, from the wicked enchantment that binds me to the dust and allows me to see the sun only once every thousand years."

"I hope so, indeed," said Finn. "My thanks to you, O Thrig of Tone. Perhaps I can return the favor one day. Farewell."

And he went piping off through the woods, followed by various beasts.

But it's not so easy to get away with a good deed in this spinning egg of a world. Evil has lidless eyes and does not sleep. At the very moment that Finn was ending his lesson, Drabne of Dole, deep in her hole, a thousand miles down, was gazing into a hand mirror, combing her snaky hair with the backbone of a fish. Then the mirror darkened; she could not see herself. And she knew that somewhere on earth a good deed was being born. For good, the mere breath of it, always darkened her mirror. She gnashed her teeth and stamped her foot, crying:

Oh grief, oh woe,
I'll not have it,
No, no, no . . .
Not a shred of kindness,
Nor a ray of joy . . .
I'll bend him, rend him,
Tame him, maim him,
Whatever he be,
Large or wee,
Man or boy . . .

So saying, she flapped her bat-wing sleeves and flew a thousand miles in a wink of an eye to the old oak tree where the Thrig of Tone stood gazing after Finn. She snatched him up and stuffed him into her purse, and flew back a thousand miles to her den.

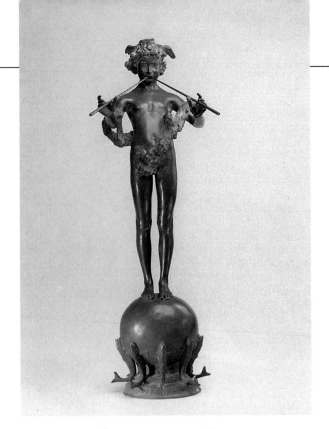

*And he went piping off
through the woods . . .*

She put him on the stool where she sat to do her sewing, bound him with thread, and stabbed him with a needle, crooning:

Stab and jab
jab and stab . . .
Better talk,
better gab . . .

"No," groaned the thrig.

"Been doing good deeds again, haven't you? Let you out of my sight for a minute every thousand years, and up you pop into the light trying to help some poor fool do the right thing instead of taking life as it is. Well, you'll tell me what you did, and I'll undo it."

"Never," said the thrig.

"Never's a long time, little one, especially when there's pain attached. You'll tell me, for I'll torment you till you do."

> I come and I go,
> I fly and I spy.
> I am Drabne of Dole,
> I live in a hole,
> and I need to know. . . .

"That's what witch means, small fool, Woman Who Knows. Now hear what I intend, Thrig of Tone: If you don't tell me straight, I'll round off your edges a bit and use you as a pincushion for the next ten hundred years. And it'll be pain, pain, pain all the time. I have plenty of tatters that need mending. My master's socks need doing too. His hooves, you know, they wear right through."

Thereupon she poked and prodded and jabbed and stabbed the poor little fellow until he could bear it no longer, and told her what he had done.

"Aha," she said. "A very good deed, indeed, but not too late to stop."

She threw him into her workbasket and stomped off to her big iron pot, where it boiled over a fire of brambles. She cast in the scale of a fishy thing that lives at the bottom of the sea and has neither sight nor touch nor any sense at all but is one blind suck. Henbane she added, and nightshade, wormwood, drear weed, and various poison fats that clog the senses, whispering all the while:

> In this cauldron
> Stew and roast.
> Hearing ail,

Music fail,
Make him then
Deaf as post. . . .

A smoke arose from the witch's brew, curling in the spirals of a most evil spell, and wafted itself out of her den and up the long way into the world—flew into the wood and fumed around the flat head of one of the serpents who was following Finn, drawn by his music. This serpent straightaway fell deaf, heard nothing anymore, but followed along anyway, no longer dancing, only crawling, filling with stupefied wrath.

Finn knew nothing. He went skipping and piping through the wood until he came to his own village, silent now, for it was the hot, golden after-lunch hour when giants nap. He climbed into his bull-hide cradle and gazed upon young Murtha, sleeping sweetly as a folded flower.

"Sleep, little beauty," he whispered. "Sleep, my flower. Dream whatever dreams you do, and I shall sit here and my music shall steal through your ears and into your dreams, and when you awake you will hear the same music and not know whether you are awake or asleep, seeing me or dreaming still. And when the snakes come and frighten you, it will be with the slowness of nightmare, and in the darkened enchantment of that half dream you will hear me play and see me do, and watch the writhing evil dance to my tune. So you will know me for what I am and love me forever. Sleep then, sleep until you awake."

He sat cross-legged and began to pipe again. The wolves came, and the deer. Bear, fox, badger, rabbit, weasel. They stood at the foot of the tree, listening. Then, sure enough, he saw the serpents unreeling themselves through the branches of the tree, winding down toward the cradle.

"Strange," he thought to himself, "they were mottled green, both of them, but now one has changed color. It's a dull gray, like lead. Oh, well, I suppose he has changed his skin.

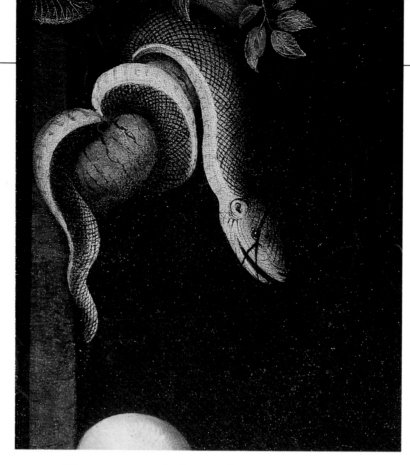

*Then, sure enough, he saw the serpents unreeling
themselves through the branches of the tree,
winding down toward the cradle.*

Snakes do, I hear. What's the difference? I'll play and they shall dance."

The green snake was already dancing, slowly winding fold upon mottled fold about the limb from which the cradle swung. But the gray one had crawled into the cradle itself, filling it with great coils of dully glimmering metal hide.

Murtha was awake now, staring with stark-wide violet eyes at what had come into her sleep. And Finn thought that he was locked in nightmare. For this snake was not dancing. Its tiny eyes were poison red and seemed to be spinning, making Finn's head whirl with fear. Not dancing, this serpent, but oozing toward Finn. It curled the tip of its tail around the lad's ribs and began to squeeze. Finn felt his bones cracking. He could do nothing else, so he kept playing. He sat there piping, although the breath was being choked out of him. As his sight darkened he saw the snake above still dancing. And Finn, knowing that he was being killed, put all his pain and all his fear and all his loneliness into the pipe, and the pipe answered.

Now the green snake above danced on, filled with the wild, sleepy magic of this music. The last exquisite strains of Finn's fluting plaited the snake's loops with slow joy, so that the coils he wove were made of living cable, stronger than steel. And when he heard the music growing dim and saw the gray serpent throttling Finn, he simply cast a loop about the strangler and pressed the life out of its body, all without ceasing his dance.

Finn felt the coils lose their deathly grip; his breath came free. In the huge joy of breathing he blew so loud a blast upon his reed that the giants awoke and came running to see. What they saw was young Finn sitting in his bull-hide cradle piping a tune, and a huge green serpent dancing, and another metal-colored snake hanging limp and dead, while violet-eyed little Murtha shook her shoulders and snapped her fingers and smiled like the sun upon water.

"Finn!" cried his mother, snatching him up and hugging him to her. "Are you all right? Has the murdering beast harmed you, my child?"

"I'm fine, Mother. Put me back and let me play."

Finn's mother was not much for weeping, but she wept then.

"Don't cry, Mother. Take the silver one and skin off his hide and make yourself a belt."

"I'll do that, Son. And know it for the finest girdle in all the world."

The giants were whispering to each other. "'Tis a wonder now. A proud mother she is this day. Young Finn's a hero for all his small bones."

"Save a bit of the hide to make a drum for Murtha here," said Finn. "Do that, Mother, and she will drum to my fluting and all will be well."

"Do it I will," said his mother. "As soon as the beast can be peeled."

"Answer me, darlin'," said Finn to Murtha. "Will you have a silver drum and beat the measure as I play?"

The giants shouted their pride. The animals brayed and bellowed and trumpeted. A muffled shriek of pain came from Drabne of Dole, for witches suffer when wickedness fails. And the birds in the trees made a racket of glee.

The giants then began to stamp too,
stomping the earth mightily . . .

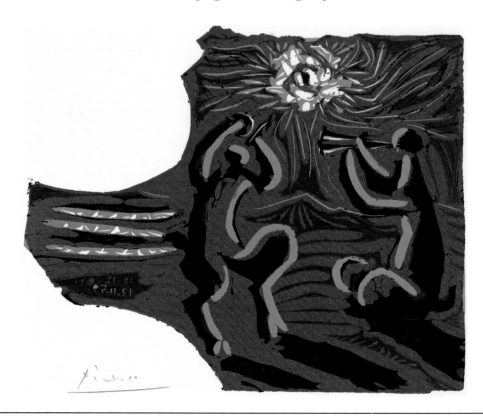

Young Murtha, though, said nothing at all; she wasn't one for answering questions. Besides, she was doing something new. She stood among the snake's coils and danced along with him. He swayed, casting his green loops about her like a garland come to life. The giants then began to stamp too, stomping the earth mightily, shaking the trees.

And Drabne of Dole, deep underground, whimpered and moaned and screamed, but no one heard her, for the day was full of joyful noise.

As for the Thrig of Tone, the witch's grief was his chance. He undid his bonds and escaped from her workbasket and made his way back to the wood. There he lives till this day, they say, doing sometimes good and sometimes mischief according to his mood, but mostly good nowadays, for the balance is so much the other way.

Children still get lost in that wood, and when they are found, say that a manikin with a face like a nut taught them to take music out of a reed. He wears a crown, they say, which is a single crystal, tear shaped, full of moon fire. Their parents laugh and tell them they were never lost at all but only asleep, dreaming. The children do not argue, but they know what they know. And it's a fact that children so lost and so found grow up fond of strange places and adventure. They go about the world confusing wind and laughter, tears and moon crystals, teasing music out of reeds, heroes out of shadows, stories out of grief.

2

The Fish Hag

o the young Finn had balked Drabne of Dole in her first attempt on his life. But she was not one to be comfortably defied; she fed on foundered dreams and drank young tears like wine. What was worse, she was a two-day witch. When not being Drabne she doubled as the Fish Hag.

And as the Fish Hag she had a job to do in the scheme of things. She guarded the Salmon of Knowledge to see that this important fish was not hooked by the wrong people, or things learned by those who were meant to be ignorant. It was a hard job. Many there were who hunted the Salmon—Ireland has always been a land of scholars—and the Fish Hag had little time for tormenting a frisky lad. But she loathed Finn enough to take on extra work. And she began to set out baits for him.

She studied him awhile from hidden places and found that he belonged to that curious breed whose weaknesses do not matter because they are most surely betrayed by their gifts. Now Finn had many gifts, but they were still raw. An imagination that darkened the horses of the sun for night use so that they galloped through his sleep, bearing him to certain hills and valleys where he knew he had been before. This was a gift, but raw. For he insisted on searching for these hills and valleys and green-lit meadows and echoing caves even when he was awake, and could not accept it when they were not to be found. Also, from the first, he suffered from fear of being a coward, pushing himself to rash acts that were to pass for courage. And this trait of his was useful to Drabne, but she needed something else—and found it in his feeling for Murtha, which was his most perilous gift. For he was too young to be doing what he was doing, and that was attaching the idea of all grace and surprise to the image of one girl.

Upon a summer day then, Murtha, while wandering in a wood, heard a hoarse voice speak her name.

"Murtha, Murtha . . ."

"Who calls me?"

"Myself."

"Where are you?"

"Not where you're looking. Lift your eyes."

Murtha looked up. There, seated on a low limb of an alder tree, was an ugly gray bird with a pouchy beak.

"Good morning to you," said Murtha. "What sort of bird do you call yourself?"

"Pelican."

"Why is your beak made like that?"

"For carrying fish back to my nest."

"Are you a fishing bird, then?"

"Am I not? The very best."

"What do you do so far from the sea? There are no fish here."

"I have come to see you, Murtha."

"Well, that's friendly of you. How is it you can talk at all, by the way? Is it common among pelicans?"

"Not very. But I'm a special bird, if I say so myself. I'm not only good at speaking but at guessing. I know, for instance, what you would like best in the world—an opal necklace with stones as big as hazelnuts, full of drowned lights."

"The very thing!" cried Murtha, clapping her hands. "I didn't know what it was I wanted most in the world, but now that you've mentioned it I can't wait till I get one."

"And I'm here to tell you how," said the pelican, who was really Drabne, or the Fish Hag in disguise, of course. "A bit of a way it is, past three meadows and a wood, up one hill and down two to a secret place. There stand nine hazels circling a spring. At the bottom of that spring is a bed of opals. . . . Here must Finn McCool come in the first dawn, and if he asks me courteously, I will tell him how to dive for those opals, and you shall have a necklace finer far than any worn by any princess of any realm."

"I'll come get them myself. I can swim and dive better than Finn."

"No, it must be he."

"Oh, pooh. Why?"

"It is the way of things. The jewel a girl wears must be given her by a lad or it loses its luster. Now don't be wasting my time. Do you want those opals or not?"

"Oh, yes."

"Then go tell Finn what to do. Off with you!"

"Thank you, Mr. Pelican."

"*Miss*, dear. But you are welcome indeed."

The pelican rose heavily and flapped away. And Murtha, seeing the ragged wings and the stiff tail and the humped beak, felt her heart squeezed by fear, for it seemed the shape of a witch riding a broomstick and not a bird at all. But then she saw the opals sliding their lights about the slenderness of her neck, and she forgot her fear and ran off to tell Finn.

Just as the windy sky showed its first apricot glow, Finn McCool came to the place he had been told to go, past three meadows and a wood, up one hill and down two. There he counted nine hazels huddled in the mist about a spring of water. There was a

*Upon a summer day . . . , Murtha, while wandering
in a wood, heard a hoarse voice
speak her name.*

curdling of the mist as the boy watched; it thickened into the
shape of a hag, who said:

"A fair morning to you, boy-dear."

"The like to you, mistress."

"And what brings you to the Spring of the Nine Hazels,
Finn?"

"I was instructed to come here."

"Indeed? And who did the instructing, may I ask?"

"Murtha of the Vale."

"Murtha, is it? How does she know of this place, and by what right does she tell you what she knows?"

"She was advised by a pelican to tell me to come here and fetch her the opals that lie beneath the stream."

"Pelicans, opals, little girls who know more than what's good for them and little boys who know less. This is a mixed-up tale you're telling me, and I don't like it at all."

The crone wore a tattered cloak. She had wild feathery gray hair and hands like the feet of a bird. Her nose bent to meet her chin and the chin curved up to meet the nose halfway. Every time she spoke both nose and chin moved, and Finn was so fascinated waiting to see whether they would finally touch that he lost the drift of her words.

"Why are you looking at me in that foolish way?"

"I am waiting to see whether your nose touches your chin. It comes closer each word. It's very interesting."

"Is it, now?"

She smiled and Finn shuddered. Ugly as she was in the ordinary way, the look of her trying to be pleasant was not to be believed.

"Pray be not displeased, mistress. I meant no rudeness."

"Oh, you have a few lessons in courtesy to learn, but time enough, time enough. I have so much to teach you I don't know where to start."

"Are you a teacher?"

"Not by trade. But every good mistress instructs her own servants."

"I am no servant. I am Finn McCool."

"The very name I was given. Enough chatter, though. Lessons are bitter here, and the first of them is 'Shut up and listen.' "

He leaped away and started to run. She pointed her hands at him, muttering. A sewing basket floated in out of nowhere and perched between her hands. She continued muttering. A spool leaped out of the basket, rolled rapidly along the ground, hopping over twigs, and circled Finn, casting its threads about him, binding his legs. Though delicate as silk, the thread was strong as cable; he could not move. The spool rose in the air, still circling, and wrapped him about until he was cocooned from shoulder to foot. The witch whistled. The spool sailed back into the basket and paused to allow a needle to thread itself. The needle flashed out of the basket toward Finn. Darting more swiftly than a dragonfly, it sewed up his lips.

"The less you speak the more you hear. And for a learner, listening is a lot better than discussion," said Drabne. "Any questions? No? Splendid. You've learned something already."

Finn felt his eyes fill with hot tears, but they were of rage, not grief. And when he thought the witch would misread them, he grew angrier than ever, and the hot tears gushed.

"Yes, weep," said the hag. "You'll learn it won't help, so you'll stop. Oh, I know it's painful, but pain is the beginning of education." She snapped her fingers. "Needle, thread, your work is done. Come back home, the lesson's begun."

The thread binding Finn was drawn back into the humming spool in the witch's basket, and the needle flashed back to its cushion. And now something truly fearful arose from the basket, a scissors flying like a bird, snapping its steel beak. The scissors-bird darted in on Finn, nipped his ear till the blood came. Finn picked up a stick and batted at it, but the scissors-bird was far too quick and flashed in and out lightly, sticking and nipping the boy until he felt as though he had been rolled in nettles. He dropped his stick and the scissors stopped biting, but sailed close to his head, snapping its jaws.

"He will be your tutor," said Drabne. "He is called the Scholar's Friend. He will keep you up to the mark."

So Finn became the Fish Hag's servant and learned certain duties about the pool. Simple ones at first. To feed small worms

"A fair morning to you, boy-dear."

to larger ones until the larger ones grew fat enough to be fed to the Salmon, whom Finn never saw plain, only as a silver flash when he rose at dusk to feed. Finn was taught to hunt plump tadpoles for the fish, and to peel them before casting them back into the pool.

"Truly, he's a delicate feeder, this fellow," said Finn to himself. "And I should not mind having a look at him at all."

For something had happened to Finn in his few weeks of servitude. He had grown used to pain and hard work and even to his fear of the circling scissors–bird and the hovering hag. He had gotten used to his lips being sewed up tight. Since he could not speak with anyone else, he held long, interesting conversations with himself. Indeed, tuned to listening as he was, and forced to take note of things as his painful lessons multiplied, he found himself growing more curious, needing to know how things worked, how they came to be, how they connected with other things. His biggest pain was the sense of being compelled to act in a certain way without his own wishes being consulted. He could not bear the idea of being considered a servant. But he found that concocting silent plans of vengeance, vividly pictured, enacted in great detail before sleep, helped him to forget that pain too. So he lulled himself each night with charades of violence done to Drabne, to the faithful denizens of her workbasket, to the Salmon, which he still knew only as a silver flash at dusk.

But then upon a day he was instructed to change the Salmon's diet. Preparations were under way for the great night of the year, the night of the midsummer moon, when the Druids were to assemble from far and near to eat of the Salmon, whose flesh would be magically renewed, and, having eaten, to return to their places with bellies full of wisdom to last the year. So worms and tadpoles were stricken from the menu. Now all the Salmon fed upon were the hazelnuts shaken from the nine hazels. To Finn's surprise he was not instructed to crack the nuts, only to shake the trees so that the hard little bolls fell into the stream. He wondered about this.

And Drabne, who sometimes, disquietingly, seemed able to read his thoughts, said, "In these nuts lie kernels of wisdom. When such are to be swallowed, why, then the jaws of the eater must be strong enough to crack the shells for himself."

Finn stole a nut and tried to crack it between his teeth. It was like chewing a pebble; all he did was give himself a toothache. "Seems there's no shortcuts to these matters," he said to himself. "Well, I must look sharp, then—to steal myself a taste of the Salmon when the Druids feast. For, sure, I must learn enough at least to get myself free of this place and leave my mark on those who have done me harm."

Now, by this time the scissors-bird had snipped the thread binding Finn's lips; it was understood that he had lost the habit of idle speech, and had learned to listen. Indeed, there was little time for anything but preparations for the Druid feast. Three times each day he had to shake the nine hazels so that they would spill their nuts upon the stream, and the Salmon now struck the surface often to feed, not only at dusk. Finn admired the long, lithe thrust of him. Smoothly armored in silver he was; like living coals dusted with ashes were the eyes in their flat sockets. When he opened his mouth it was full of glittering knives. All gullet he seemed, and the Fish Hag chanted:

"Look sharp, look sharp. Nothing is as hungry as wisdom, for everything must feed it, even hunger. So shake the tree, lad, shake it hard."

That night Finn could not sleep. He left the little kennel where he slept behind the witch's cottage, and drifted over the meadow through the grove of trees circling the pool. The scissors-bird flew sentry as he wandered, not bothering to drive him back toward his hutch, just keeping watch lest he try to escape. Finn sat on the bank staring at the pool. It was black as a tar pit. Then

He dropped his stick and the scissors stopped biting, but sailed close to his head, snapping its jaws.

he saw a gliding sliver of light, and he did not know whether the moon was throwing darts from a chink in the clouds or whether it was the Salmon rising.

"It must be the moon," he thought. "The Salmon lies far below, fast asleep."

He heard a voice say, "Good evening, Finn."

"Good evening, sir."

"Are you sad, lad?"

"I cannot sleep."

"Then you are too happy or too sad. And I do not believe you are happy."

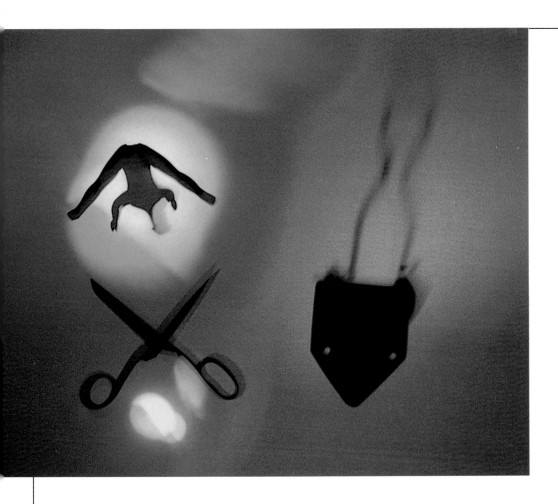

"True for you, Master Salmon."

"You're not old enough to be sad, Finn."

"What age do you have to be?"

"Old enough to have seen enough and done enough to have earned the right. What you think is sadness are silly little vapors of discontent, because you are not man enough to do what you have to do."

"Which is what?"

"Why, to free yourself, of course. To destroy your enemies and help your friends."

"You make it sound simple. I don't know where to begin."

"At the beginning, lad. Where else?"

"And what is that?"

"Name your enemy."

"Oh, that's easy. Drabne and her helpers—especially the scissors-bird."

"Very well; they'll do for a start. Destroy them, and your immediate troubles will be over, and you'll be ready for the next batch."

"But how? The Fish Hag is very powerful. She has magic on her side—flying needles, spools of thread that tie you up before you know what's happening, and that terrible shears so swift and sharp, who can cut a lad to pieces as if he were a bolt of cloth."

"I'm sorry, Finn," said the Salmon. "I seldom give advice. And when I do, it's along general lines. No details. But seeing as you are rather young and tender and may do some interesting things if you are permitted to live, I will stretch a point and tell you this: When faced by powerful enemies, son, use their own weapons against them. Use their strength to your advantage. Seek your allies in the very heart of their camp."

"I'm sure that's good policy, sir," said Finn. "But I still don't know how to go about it. Dole me out a bit of your magic wisdom, pray. Just one detail or two of real practical instruction."

"Why, for that, Finn, I would need more than your need. The only way you can learn such of me is not by questioning but by eating of my flesh, the way the Druids do."

"But I am not a Druid, and if I steal from them, I will be punished most horribly, the witch has said. She will put me to the Fire Flick and the Marrow Log."

"Yes. Secrets and penalties, risks and rewards all go together, Finn. Farewell."

He flipped in the air and dived and the water closed blackly over him.

"Well, some of it sounded like good advice," said Finn to himself. "If I can just figure how to use it."

Finn sat on the bank, staring at the pool.

He went back to his hutch and slept. But the next morning he wasn't so sure. It's tricky being advised by moonlight; he did not know whether he had actually been conversing with the wise Salmon or whether it had all been a dream. Suppose it had? Wisdom was sometimes offered in dream scenes; the old stories were full of it. Besides, he was never quite certain of how much he saw in his sleep and how much elsewhere.

But something had changed in him all the same. He found himself doing the first thing that came into his head, and that was a peculiar thing. Druids were gathering in the grove. They were clad in green—long, beautiful, leaf green robes from which their clean, gnarled faces shone. And Finn could see how they had come to be known as Tree Priests, Sages of the Mistletoe. When they doffed their robes for a ceremonial wetting in the pool, Finn crept among the scattered garments, swiftly ripping each one. When the Druids emerged, dripping, and began to dress, there was a great outcry. Their beards shook with rage; they scolded like great jays, grew hoarse as crows, cursing. And Finn was pleased to see Drabne turn into their servant, scurry among them trying to appease them, vowing she would sew up every rip so that they would never know it was mended.

She squatted right there on the bank of the pool with her workbasket on her lap and began to mend, needle swiftly flashing in and out of the green cloth swaddled about her. The scissors-bird swooped away from its perch near Finn and dived into the workbasket to be ready when the hag needed to snip. Now Finn had his enemy and her helpers busy doing something else. He left the pool and ran beyond the hazel copse to the witch's cottage. It was the Sacred Salmon Net he was after, and he had to move fast.

The eyes of the Fish Hag's cat cast the only light in the room, but Finn lit no candle; he wanted it dark for his deed. Well he knew what dreadful punishments lay in store for him if he should be caught—just thinking of the Fire Flick and the Marrow Log was enough to scare a lad into obedience, and right then and there he almost gave up his plan. But then the voice of the hag creaked in his ears saying, "Do this . . . do that . . ." and he thrust aside his fears and whistled the cat to him. The big black tom leaped to his shoulder. Finn felt its purr boiling beneath his hand as he twisted the cat's head now this way, now that, so he could see by the light of its blazing green eyes. The cat loved Finn, who, in his deepest trouble, found time to tease him with a dangled string and to toss him a peeled tadpole now and then.

Now, the Sacred Salmon Net had come down from the earliest mists of time when the magic kings of the Tuatha da Danaan reigned in Ireland. Fashioned by Giobniu, the great smith, it was spun of the beard of Mamos, the first Druid, and its handle was a rod of gold. When Finn snatched it off the shelf it seemed no implement at all but a living extension of his own arm, and he knew he could scoop up any swimming thing from any water in the world.

Swiftly he left the cottage, bearing the net. Swiftly he circled the meadow where the Druids were matching verse while the witch was mending, then darted through the hazel copse to the edge of the pool. And then, instead of dipping the net, stood there panting, watching the stars float upside down.

Finn stood at the edge of the pool; it seemed like a gulf of shadow waiting to swallow him. He stood there at the edge of wisdom, between boyhood and manhood, and was taken by a creeping, bloodsucking sadness in which Murtha's face hung, now laughing, now cruel, garlanded by memory. And he stood there trying to fight the sadness and let the laughter and cruelty enter him. He felt himself fill with a choking excitement. Now? he asked the night. Now! said the Salmon Net. Now! sighed the trees. Now! sang the drowning stars, and Finn dipped his net.

He needed but one dip. The net had barely grazed the water

when the Salmon flashed out, curved in the air, and landed in the mesh. Finn felt the net come alive with the sudden weight of the great fish. It twitched out of his hands. He bellowed with rage and smote his head.

"Easy, Finn. Don't go breaking your skull like that—with so many others ready to do it for you."

Finn looked about for the voice and saw the Salmon standing on the shore wearing the net like a cape.

"Enough gawking, lad. You've caught me, now do it."

"How shall I cook you, sir?"

"No time for cooking."

"What do you mean?"

"I'm to be taken raw. Knowledge doesn't have to be palatable; it just has to be swallowed. And if you cannot stomach the truth unflavored, why, then you're not meant to be wise."

"But I am," said Finn.

Then, at the edge of the pool in the weird pearly light of the midsummer moon, Finn ate the Salmon from nose to tail—flesh, bone, scales, guts, eyes—he ate every bit, and a terrible, griping, slimy meal it was. No sooner had he swallowed the last of it than he jumped into the pool, clothes and all, to wash himself clean. When he climbed back onto the bank there stood the Salmon, taller than Finn, looking like a prince in his close-fitting armor of silver.

"Now, Finn," he said. "I will tell you what you need to know."

"How do I escape the hag?"

"Your first problem is this: Having been eaten once, I am no longer available for the Druid feast, and our bearded friends are getting hungrier and hungrier. Listen, you can hear them railing at the witch."

Finn listened, and heard an angry chattering.

"I hear them. Where is she?"

The net had barely grazed the water
when the salmon flashed out,
curved in the air . . .

"At the cottage searching for the Salmon Net and not finding it. It won't take her long to figure out who stole it."

"What shall I do, wise sir? What shall I do?"

"Dip the net again. Catch the Loutish Trout."

"But the Druids have been eating salmon flesh for nine hundred years now. Surely they know the difference between salmon and trout."

"Not if you follow this recipe: Baste the trout in vinegar and butter, parsley, scallions. Dust it with wheat crumbs and crumbled mandragore. Then lay strips of bacon upon it and broil it until the skin is charred. Stuff it with sautéed crabmeat and serve with a sauce of almonds seethed in cream and sprinkled with poppy. Can you remember that?"

"Yes, sir."

"Do it, and so delicious will it be that the Druids will forget all distinction between salmon and trout, loutishness and wisdom, for they will be too busy cramming their gullets with both hands. Then, with bellies full and the drowsy fumes of mandragore and poppy working, they will fall into a sleep so heavy nothing will wake them before breakfast."

"What of Drabne?"

"Oh, she will partake of the feast too, and will grow drowsy enough for you to strike a blow—that is, if you have followed my recipe, selected each ingredient, and done your frying and broiling for the proper time."

"What of the scissors-bird?"

"You'll have to handle him on your own. But quickly now, lad, or you'll flub the whole matter. Get cracking with that net and catch the Loutish Trout."

"Wait!" cried Finn. "I have questions to ask."

"No time left. I'll give you an all-purpose answer. To break a curse, make a verse."

And he disappeared.

Again Finn dipped his net and again snared a fish—quite a different one this time, a fat trout with a speckled belly and a foolish face.

Finn cooked the trout as instructed, following the Salmon's recipe exactly. And exactly then did events befall as the wise fish had foretold. The Druids fell upon the savory dish and devoured it with gusto, smacking their lips and licking their fingers; and no sooner had each finished his portion than he stretched upon the grass in the deepest sleep he had ever slept, and the glade filled with the great snuffling drone of their snores.

Drabne had eaten heavily of the trout too, but when she felt herself slipping into sleep, she knew that Finn had been taught to trick her. Summoning all her uncanny will she propped herself against a tree and with her last strength began to mutter into her workbasket.

Finn, seeing her do this, knew that he would soon be attacked by a swarm of needles and pins, not to mention the terrible scissors-bird. He could not outrace them, he could not hide from them, he could not ward off their agonizing stings. Then the last words of the Salmon came to him. To break a curse, make a verse. And just as the shining swarm began to rise from the basket, he shouted:

> Needle and pin,
> So bright and thin,
> And sharp as sin,
> Put a stitch
> In Mistress Witch;
> Sew nose to chin,
> And chin to tree.
> Heed young Finn,
> He'll set you free . . .

And, not believing his own power, he watched in ballooning joy as the needles and pins turned in midair and flashed toward the warty face of the witch. Swerving in bright patterns, the pins basted her chin to the tree, and the needles sped after, trailing thread, and made it permanent. But then something sliced through Finn's joy; it was the scissors-bird rising viciously out of the basket, and, try as he might, Finn could not find a verse to turn this terror. He did not have to. . . . The one verse was enough. For the faithful scissors-bird snapped about his mistress, trying to cut the threads that bound her to the tree. As fast as he cut them, the needles sewed them up again.

As his enemies were thus occupied, Finn strode away from the pool, through the hazel copse, and across the glade where he had suffered much and learned more. Nor did he walk alone. Winners seldom do. The witch's cat leaped upon his shoulder and perched there like a heavy shadow, grinning wickedly at the squirrels and greening his eyes at troubled birds.

It was this huge black tom that Finn tried to give Murtha as a gift.

"Keep your cat," she said. "It was opals you promised, and opals I must have."

"I'll keep looking," said Finn.

But if Murtha gained nothing from that adventure, Finn was given something very important; the Salmon had shown him the beginnings of wisdom. Only the beginning, but enough to go on with. The Salmon's final words to him were:

"It may be that you will seek my counsel when I am too far away to answer you. In such case I shall speak through the Harp of Dagda, whose song you shall be able to understand."

"What is this Harp of Dagda?"

"You will know when it comes. It shall appear to you only at the moment of greatest peril."

"Well," said Finn. "In my short career, peril has not been in short supply. I have an idea I shall be needing your counsel soon again."

"Let us await the occasion," said the Salmon.

"Waiting . . ." murmured Finn. "That's the thing I do worst."

"And the thing that will serve you best," said the Salmon. "But you will learn, lad. It's the hardest lesson of all, but you will learn. . . ."

3

The Winter Burning

he King of Ireland lay asleep in his castle at Tara. Behind huge stone walls he slept, and the antechambers were full of armed men; even so, a dream slipped by.

He was awakened by the sound of his own voice, bellowing. Sword in hand, the royal guards rushed in.

"I do not want you," said the king. "Here is a threat beyond violence. Send for my Druids."

The Druids came and the king told his dream.

"A young lad walks along a shore I have never seen, but I know it is near. His hair is so black it seems blue and his eyes so blue they look black. He is attended by a fish in armor and a tomcat larger than a terrier. He stops to look upon the skeleton of a whale. The wind blows through the ribs, making a battle music; the boy sings with it, sings words of menace and mirth as the waves dance and the fish jigs on its tail and the cat bows and the moon wobbles in a ghastly dance. . . . Read me the dream then, O men of wisdom."

The Druids deliberated among themselves, beards wagging. The eldest spoke:

"Know this, High King, your dream is but the last in a

series of signs that tell of a doomful event—the coming of Finn McCool."

"The name means nothing to me."

"Finn McCool, son of Cuhal, leader of the Fianna, murdered by old Morna, whose sons enjoy your favor."

"Son of Cuhal, is he? And why was not the wolf-whelp killed along with his father?"

"His mother hid him."

"Was no search made?"

"High and low, over, under, middle, and across. But she hid him well."

"And was it young Finn I saw in my dream?"

"Himself. It was a prophetic dream you had—as the best kings do—so that you might prepare yourself."

"Does he dare come here so young and ungrown to avenge his father and claim the leadership of the Fianna?"

"He does so."

"Shall I fear the boy?"

"You shall. He has learned of the Salmon and knows things it is well for one's foe not to know. You must arm yourself, King. A living enemy has stepped out of the colored shadows of your sleep."

So the High King of Ireland prepared himself against the coming of Finn, and plotted deeply with the sons of Morna. Now by the Law of Hospitality the boy could not be killed while a guest at the castle, nor upon the road to it. The trick then would be to make him quit the court by his own choice, for the law also said that a guest might not be forced to leave—but once having left the king's table he was fair game and could be sent to join his father upon the unthawable ice fields that lie in the Darkness Beyond Night.

"What we must do is make him *want* to leave," said the king to Goll McMorna, eldest of the cruel, beautiful sons of Morna.

"What we must do is make him want *to leave."*

"Well, let us think now," said Goll. "If he was tutored by
the Salmon he will know full well that he is protected by the
Law of Hospitality, and will leave only if it becomes too uncomfortable for him to stay."

"The law also says he cannot be forced to leave."

"Who speaks of forcing? We will merely introduce him to
an experience or two that no lad of mettle would care to miss.

If the sport becomes too rough or an accident befalls—well, no blame can attach to us, for we shall have warned him."

"You speak in riddles, Goll. How can we warn him against danger and still lead him to it?"

"If he be the true son of Cuhal, O King, then he will be ridden by a pride that will gall him bloody if he shows fear. I remember well how his father rode straight into our ambush, knowing that we couched there in our strength, but scorning to turn tail on a fight though he be outnumbered ten to one. Yes, for this son of Cuhal, our warnings will serve as a joyous summons to a fatal task."

Castles then were not so grimly gray as they were later to become. The walls of Tara were cut out of a white cliff; its roof was striped crimson and blue. Chariots circled the walls, carrying two warriors each. They were drawn by matched stallions. Finn, seeing this blaze of color for the first time, forgot about his murdered father and his plans for vengeance and gawked happily at the tall young charioteers whose hair streamed in the speed of their going. And the magnificent war stallions took the rest of his breath, for if there was one thing Finn esteemed above any other, it was a handsome animal—man, woman, dog, or horse.

As the lad stood staring at the bright chariots, a man strolled up holding a falcon, not on his wrist as falconers do, but perched on his shoulder. This pleased Finn because the man had a hawk face himself and it was like seeing a man with two heads. Now riding on Finn's shoulder was Drabne's black tom, who accompanied the lad everywhere since breaking with the witch. The man looked down at the boy. The falcon glared down at the cat, who swelled with rage, arching his back and greening his eyes. Finn laughed.

"Something amuse you?" said the man.

"Much amuses me, sir." said Finn. "I am easily entertained."

"Are you, now? But perhaps I do not care to be laughed

at by a raw cub, whose name, estate, and parentage I do not know."

"My name is Finn McCool. I am my father's son, as will be disclosed to those who knew him last. As for my estate, this I must discuss with the High King."

"And do you think the High King can listen to every vagabond who turns off the road?"

"No, sir. But to Finn McCool, yes."

"Is there something special about you, Master McCool?"

"I cannot tell. I am the only one of me I know."

"I have the liveliest kind of wish to beat you until you cannot walk," said the tall man.

"I'm sorry to hear that," said Finn.

"You'd be sorrier yet, my lad, if you were not shielded by the Law of Hospitality."

"Seems a pity that a man like you should be balked by a little thing like a law," said Finn.

"Do not mock me," gritted the man.

"I know how you must feel not being able to beat me," said Finn. "I see that you are a man of splendid wrath. I see the flaming coils of it springing from your head."

Now, it was a deadly insult at that time to refer to anyone's physical appearance, unless it were a lover, chieftain, or closest kin, or any combination of these. And Finn knew that he was walking a knife edge. He was trying to provoke the man to attack, of course; for, without knowing the redhead's name, he had recognized him immediately as a final foe whom he must either destroy or be destroyed by. And since he was too young to engage him in physical combat, Finn was trying to goad him into losing his temper and violating the Law of Hospitality, thus incurring the death penalty.

Such was Finn's plan, but, observing the man's face gone suddenly cheese white, and the huge writhing fingers, Finn saw that he might have gone too far, that he might have let himself in for immediate annihilation, which was not part of his plan at all. For the boy had met enemies before—snakes and hags and all the sore magic blades in a witch's kit—but he had never yet angered mortal man, and he was amazed to see how totally savage was this wrath, lighted by intelligence, more urgent than hunger, closer than breathing.

The man said nothing at all; his fingers now were playing with the ankle gyve of the bird. The huge falcon rose suddenly from the man's shoulder, soared until it was blotted in the gray brightness, then dived. It dropped out of the sky in a heavy,

The man said nothing at all;
his fingers now were playing with
the ankle gyve of the bird.

46

screaming stoop straight for Finn's head. He looked up. Gaffing down upon him were the wicked hooks that could tear the heart out of an arctic goose in midflight. Bigger than the sky, they came clutching for his head.

The cat on Finn's shoulder yawned, flicking its coral tongue, grinning right into the hooks of death—then rose straight up to meet the diving falcon. Finn watched aghast, expecting to see his pet, twice beloved because taken from an enemy, smashed into a bloody rag of fur. But he had forgotten that it was a witch's cat, witness to spells and incantations. The black tom uttered a rhymed meow and made a delicate pass with its paws. Finn saw the falcon dwindle into a wren, which had time for one flutter before the cat pulled it in, and, dropping back onto Finn's shoulder, began to chew.

"I would sooner have lost my stable of horses," said the man softly. "I took that hawk from the King of Aram after a fight that lasted three days and cost ten of my best men, not to mention a few of the worst. How shall I refrain from killing you where you stand, despite all the Laws of Hospitality ever spoken by half-witted ancients?"

"I put you under obligation," said Finn.

He said a word to the cat, who spat feathers that floated in the air, thickening into the royal shape of the falcon. The bird spread its huge wings briefly and resumed its perch on the man's shoulder.

"That's a clever cat you have there," said the man.

"He has had certain advantages," said Finn. "Now, sir, I have told you my name, will you tell me yours?"

"Goll McMorna."

"How well things fall out. You are the man I have most wanted to know, and I meet you first. You were the leader of those who killed my father, I believe."

"Still am."

"So I must kill you, of course."

"Of course you must try."

"But not quite yet. I need to grow to my full size first."

"Better grow fast," said McMorna. "That hospitality nonsense shelters you only while you are a guest here, and the Law of Obligation lasts only one year thereafter."

"Oh, but I may abide here quite a while. Tara's hospitality is famous."

"Yes, the king has been known to devise novel entertainments," said Goll, "especially for uninvited guests. Come, I'll take you to him now."

The High King made Finn welcome. Stags were roasted whole in the great fire pits of the courtyard, and young pigs, wood grouse, and pheasant turned on their spits, dripping hot gravy and giving off a smell that made the dogs howl with greed. Finn was questioned about his favorite dishes, and was served winter strawberries in clotted cream, hot chestnuts, honeycomb—and one night a fat trout cooked according to the recipe given him by the Salmon that night he had fed it to the Druids and stuffed them so full that he was able to make off with their secret wisdom.

"You need new clothes," said the king. "No son of Cuhal shall walk Tara clad like a tinker."

There was feasting every night. Bards sang stories, poets riddled, slave girls danced, acrobats turned, bears were baited, cocks fought. By day there was hunting and fishing and jousting—footraces, wrestling, puzzle verse, chess, and bowls. And all during these first days of welcome, Goll McMorna was at the king's right hand, devising pleasures for Finn.

Then, one afternoon, he and the king met secretly, and spoke in urgent whispers.

That night at the feasting the king stood on the table, banging a gold dish with his dagger.

"Silence!" he cried. "I would speak."

The voices fell off. The great dining hall filled with a silence

By day there was hunting . . .

so deep there seemed to be a humming at its core.

"Tonight is the Night of the Winter Burning," said the king. "Tonight, we fortunate ones who dwell at Tara pay our yearly toll of shame and blame and flame. Tonight we are visited by the Destroyer, and a brave man will watch, and there will be peril and pain. I need a brave man now. Who offers himself? Any man here may volunteer save Goll McMorna, whose chieftainship makes him exempt, and Finn McCool, who is too young and tender for such an adventure—and a guest besides. Speak, then. Who dares watch through the fatal night?"

Finn saw Goll smiling narrowly at him through the wavering yellow rushlight. The lad leaped to his feet, crying:

"I claim guest-gift!"

"What?" cried the king. "Now?"

"Even now."

"It is considered more courteous for a guest to take his gift when his visit ends."

"At the risk of discourtesy, O King, I must ask it now. Immediately. I cannot wait."

"What is it you wish, then? If it lies within my bounty I must grant it."

"I wish to stand watch tonight against the Dread Coming."

"Impossible!"

"Entirely possible. It lies within your bounty."

"We need a strong man to stand against the Intruder. And even so, he will perish. But at least he will have made honorable resistance. You are but a lad with no experience in battle."

"Being young is an experience in itself," said Finn. "It has given me training in being outweighed, outnumbered, and—most advantageous of all in conflict—underestimated."

Goll McMorna spoke: "It cannot be permitted, brave youth. It is certain death."

" 'Certain death' is a redundancy," said Finn. "Death is more certain than the royalty of kings, the stillness of stealth, the wisdom of good advice; it is, in fact, our prime certainty, and it is something that I, son of my father, have forbidden myself to consider. I ask your permission, King. Grant it and you are quit of guest-gift."

"Will you allow me to watch with you?" said Goll McMorna.

"What?" said Finn, smiling. "Challenge a foe, knowing myself backed by the strongest warrior in the realm? Where's the honor in that?"

All the men of the court sprang to their feet and cheered at the quickness and courtesy of his reply.

"Very well," said the king. "I have no choice. I must grant your request and make preparations for a noble wake."

Upon this Night of the Winter Burning it seemed as if all the great world beyond the castle had gathered its weathers to contribute flame. The moon burned in the black sky, casting sparks that were stars. Water glittered in fen and tarn; slippery lights danced on the waves of the sea. Hayricks smoldered in the dark fields. The moonlight fell, now silver, now green, now gold, as it fractured variously from mown grass and cope and tangled heath. Moonlight splintered upon the windows of Tara, and all the world was coldly aflame as Finn watched.

He was alone in the great council chamber. Everyone else had gone to sleep. Even the sentries had gone to sleep by order of the king, for none might await the Dread Coming save the Appointed Watcher. It was an enormous room Finn waited in. Here the king called his Druids and captains to make battle plans and to solve affairs of state. Here, although the boy did not know it, had Cuhal, his father, taken the chieftainship of the Fianna.

Weapons gleamed on the wall. The long, thick lance used for horse charge; the slender throwing javelin; the short hand spear for the hedge defense; the great two-edged sword for cutting and thrusting; the broad, short swords of the ancient iron men who, in the mists of memory, had taken land to the east, slaughtered without pity, built roads, and vanished. Harpoons of the island fighters who used the same small spear for killing men and sticking big fish. Peasant weapons for working and fighting: pitchfork, sickle, scythe, mattock, pruning hook. Weapons taken from enemies: the curved new-moon swords and horn bows of the little slant-eyed men who rode small horses on beefsteak saddles—which were also their rations—and who devoured the land like a pestilence when they rode out of the rising sun. Battle-axes and antlered helmets of the huge yellow-headed pirates who struck the coast like seahawks in their winged ships. And the enormous, long swords that took two hands to swing, called claymores, belonging to the tall Picts in the north.

Finn gazed upon these weapons. He had never yet fought with weapons. His fingers itched to hold each one, to strike with it, and to add his own trophy to the loot upon the wall. He

The moon burned in the black sky,
casting sparks that were stars.
Water glittered in fen and tarn . . .

brooded upon the weapons. Each one, he knew, held a scroll of stories, of battle and death and brave intention. He wanted to know each story and add his own. There among the weapons, like a swan among gulls, hung a harp, an ancient one by its shape. Locked in its strings, he knew, were the songs of these weapons and the men who wielded them.

By now he had almost forgotten about his mission that night and the Dread Coming. He kept staring at the harp. Each string was a thread of moonlight. The Thrig of Tone had taught him only the reed pipe, but as he stretched his fingers he could feel a current of story-music streaming between him and the harp. Then, amazed, he saw the harp slide along the wall. He dropped his hands and the harp stopped, raised them again, and the harp slid toward him. Just as he was caught up in the delight of this, something said:

"Burn! Burn!"

He whirled toward the voice. He saw a tall, cloaked figure looming blackly against the moon, which now looked in through the window in perfect fullness. The figure dropped its cloak. It was female. But difficult to see now for she was clad in a long tunic, moon colored. Her eyes were two holes and her mouth was another. Her nose was a hole. And he felt his wits slipping as her hair shook, for there was no distinction between the color of her hair and that of her face. He saw that it was not hair at all, as we know it, but strands of skin with the power of movement. It moved upon her head, separating into tentacles of flesh that curled, noosing his attention as a snake, weaving, charms a bird so it cannot move.

"Stand!" said Finn. "Name yourself."

"You know two of my names."

"Drabne?" whispered Finn, feeling himself dissolve in horror. "Fish Hag?"

"We are acquainted, you see. But not nearly so well as we shall be."

"I come to burn."

"Your errand here?" he muttered, trying to stop his bones from turning to mush.

"I come to burn," she said. "I am she who comes by night to parch all moist ideas of youth, to devour honor and courage and all their ornaments and implements, and finally, most cruel, to incinerate hope itself by my punctuality. For men know that I must come upon this night, and no matter what they do or how they pray, they cannot postpone my visit. . . . Queen of Crones am I, marrow of death, come to teach the nature of flame. What is it, young man? You like riddles. What is flame? Give me its name."

Finn said nothing. He was trying to escape the mesh of that weaving hair. Trying to struggle out of the spell cast by that voice and the words it said.

"You do not know? Then I shall teach you. Fire is impatience, deadliest of sins. Fire is despair galloping. Fire is the inevitable summoned too soon in the secret craven hollow of men, who, in their vile fear of What Must Be, bring it on too soon to ease the pain. Fire is impatience. Fire is death dancing, the music of chaos, the jewel of waste—see?"

From all the holes of her face flame gushed. Fire spurted yellow, red, and green. Tapestries burst into flame. The draft of the flame moved the weapons on the wall, making them chime, touched a string of the harp, which uttered one moaning syllable like a strong man in unutterable pain. She spat at the huge oaken council table, which fell into ash.

Then, most horrible, he saw the tentacles that were her hair coil upon themselves, and violently uncoil, springing clear off her head and hissing through the air toward him. He snatched a sword from the wall and flailed the air, cutting the tentacles into pieces as they came. Each piece, as it fell to the floor, became a flesh worm with a torch in its tail. The fiery army inched toward him as their mistress harried them onward, screaming out of her mouth-hole.

Finn could not defend himself. There was no use striking with his sword. The tentacles were cut as fine as could be. They swarmed up his legs, stinging him with their fiery tails. In his agony he sang the Final Rune taught him by the Salmon.

Creature pair of earth and air,
Here and there and everywhere,
Come, I pray, and serve me fair. . . .

No sooner had he sung that than he saw his black tomcat leap into the room. Half-blinded by smoke, he saw the great gray falcon of Goll McMorna stoop for the kill, claws gaping. Cat and hawk moved through the fiery worms like mowers through a field, slashing with tooth and claw, sweeping the meaty little gobbets into their jaws, flame and all, screaming the proud scream of rage consuming its object, growing with what it fed upon.

But the ordeal had only begun. Still confronting Finn was the tall, robed figure of his enemy, bald now, her head pocked with scorch marks, closer now. He heard the soft wordless crooning of her hate. She smiled at him. An arrow of flame seared his head and buried itself in the oaken bench, which flared brightly, fell to ash. She moved toward him. The front of his shirt caught fire.

All the contrariness of Finn gathered itself in a cold coil in his chest, freezing his flesh. He summoned up the loveliest, coldest images his short life had ever known: icy fire of cat's-eye, blue shadow of snow, turquoise wink of mountain lake, wind made visible being clothed in mist, silhouette of wild goose against the yellow moon, hard shark-smile of Norah's Shoal, and, finally, the chill tinkle of Murtha's laughter when she wanted him to know that he needed to be scorned.

The cold images clustered like snow crystals, shielding him from the darts of fire. The crone, thwarted, screamed a huge gout of flame that rolled across the floor, charring away planks, eating the beams down to the foundation stone. The floor tottered, and the whole castle spun upon its axis, whirling its shadows, scattering moonlight like the jeweled fire-tops that pampered princelings play with in the Land Beyond the Sunrise.

Finn fell to his knees, sinking beneath the heat of that hateful flame that was burning away his crystal shield. He stretched his arms toward Dagda's harp, the harp of the ancients, which hung on Tara's wall and had once belonged to the wizard bard of the Tuatha da Danaan, who sang the beginning of things, the roots of heaven and earth, in the days when the gods dawned upon the unpeopled world.

The harp flew through the air into Finn's arms. Cradling it, he played one icy plangent note, and released it. The harp flew as easily through flame as the phoenix, that marvelous bird that

Fire spurted yellow, red, and green.
Tapestries burst into flame.

lives in the heart of fire and is reborn from ash, and has become the sign of man's hope. Through net of flame flew the harp, singing icily, straight at the crone, and smote her so hard that her head was torn from her shoulders and was hurled through the window, spouting blood and fire.

The window smashed and was glued by her blood, retaining the color of flame. Lozenges of moonlight fell upon the splintered floor, healing its planks. All things arose again from fire as Finn fingered the harp and sang the phoenix song, sang each weapon and its numbered battles, which he learned through his fingers as he sang, for the harp played him even as he played it. Song of battle and deed and death, the colored fountains of youth and the parching of age. Sang past his own memory of how his father had won the chieftainship of the Fianna from the arrogant beardless youth who was now the twisted old king. And of how he, his father's son, come unto radiant triumph after the night of ordeal, would claim his own chieftainship, and begin that scroll of deeds that would become song, sung perhaps by his own son when it would be his time to sing.

The tomcat bounded in wearing scorched fur, angry, his eyes spitting green fire, and leaped upon Finn's shoulder to be comforted.

The great gray falcon flew in, feathers singed, squawking a huge oath of vengeance upon everything that moved beneath the sky, and sat on Finn's other shoulder. She and the tom were inseparable now. She had left Goll and belonged to Finn.

And Finn, stroking them, smiled to himself, remembering what the harp had told him—that he would have to take a bird and break the spell of McMorna before he would be allowed to fight Goll to the death.

He stood on the scorched grass, cradling the harp. Only the wing of the castle that held the council room where he had waited seemed to have suffered from fire. Otherwise, the walls of Tara gleamed in the moonlight—not even stained by the smoke. Finn gazed raptly at the white walls. Within waited the king, and Goll, and all the tribe of McMorna, and the rest of the brilliant court. He would go there now and tell what happened, and claim a victor's prize.

But the harp lifted in his arms and began to fly the other

way, pulling him into the open field. "Stop," said Finn. "We go to the castle now."

"No," sang the harp. "You mustn't enter."

"Why not?"

"You're preparing to do something fatally foolish."

"What?"

"If you go there now in the first flush of triumph, you will claim the chieftainship of the Fianna. In other words, you will challenge Goll. He will welcome the challenge. For he knows that if you fight him now you will lose."

"Why must I lose?"

"Because you're not ready. You are unqualified even for membership in the Fianna, let alone to lead that band of matchless warriors. So far, in your short span of years, you have done well, even very well, but for this you are not ready, not ready, not ready."

"I hear the thrice-said word; repetition does not make it more palatable. How about some details of my unreadiness?"

"Do you know what each candidate must do before being accepted in the ranks of the Fianna? Buried to the waist, and armed only with hazel stick and wicker shield, he must be able to ward off the attack of nine warriors, fully armed. Next, having defeated the nine warriors and pulled himself from the hole, he must braid up his hair and run like a fox with the Fianna in full cry after him. Through all the woods and fields of Eire must he run, from sea to sea. And if he is caught, or if a twig snaps under his foot, or one strand of his hair be disarrayed in its shining braid, then the lad has failed and will never be admitted to the band. Several other small tasks he is set: to jump from a standing position over a stick held level with his brow; to run full speed carrying sword, shield, and spear under that same stick held at the height of his knee; to run barefoot over a field of nettles—to step full upon one and receive the thorn driven into his foot without moan or murmur of pain, then, hopping, and without losing speed, to remove that thorn from his foot, and so proceed over the field."

"Impressive," said Finn. "How then shall I proceed?"

"You must come with me," said the harp. "I'll lead you across the island to a secret valley, where the McMorna will not be able to search you out and kill you. And they will try, they

He strode away from the castle,
shedding his weariness and going
at a good pace, because
the harp was pulling him.

will try. But there in that hidden place you will practice the skills of warfare. You will run and swim and leap and play with sword and spear and bow until you meet Fianna standards. Then, and not until then, you will return to this place and try those skills against your enemy."

Finn gazed at the sky; he did not answer.

"If you do not heed me now," said the harp, "if you go in there and make your claim, you will be handing Goll the easiest victory he has had since murdering your father."

"Let's go," said Finn.

He strode away from the castle, shedding his weariness and going at a good pace because the harp was pulling him. The hawk flew in slow circles above his head so as not to outdistance him. The cat prowled after, his blackness making him invisible except for the green blaze of his eyes.

4

Amara's Warrior

ow, a year later, Finn decided that he could wait no longer to challenge Goll McMorna. Although he had not yet reached his full strength, he had spent long months in weapon practice and so honed himself for battle that he could bear no further delay. So he began to journey across Meath, harp slung, sword at his side. The cat stalked after through the grass; the hawk circled low.

Finally, on a blue smoky fall day they neared Tara, castle of the High King, where Goll also dwelt, and Finn watched eagerly for the first sight of its white stone walls and its roof, striped crimson and blue. But no castle appeared. They had come to a wall of fog, not like any fog they had known; it did not move upon the wind, nor rise, nor thin away. When they tried to pass through they did not bump into anything solid, but simply lost the power of movement until they stepped back.

"What is it?" cried Finn.

"Nothingness grown solid," said the harp. "A clot of that which is not, barring that which is. Different forms of not-ness mixed, perhaps—invisibility, silence, denial—who knows what angry gods build with. Beyond lies Tara, or where Tara used to be."

"You think this the work of angry gods?"

"Or playful ones. They're equally dangerous."

"What do we do? How do we pass?"

"Hard questions. We cannot seek their answers in ordinary places. Say a verse—quickly! Touch me and sing!"

Finn touched the harp strings and sang:

Harp on tree,
Hawk to sea,
Cat makes three.

"I read it like this," said the harp. "You must hang me on a tree. The winds will come telling what they see when they blow over Meath. And you send the falcon flying to question the fowls of air. Set the creepy cat crawling in the underbrush, seeking rats and such as live in holes and burrows, going in and out and are filthy and have information. We shall gather the news and bring it back."

"Away with you, friends!" cried Finn. "And I shall study this puzzling wall more closely."

The hawk flew away to question the gulls, as instructed. The cat vanished into the underbrush. And Finn hung the harp on a willow tree.

He himself departed to circle the wall of fog and look for a way through, but he came back to where he had started without glimpsing Tara. He came to the willow tree where he had hung the harp. It swayed there in the wind, singing softly. The hawk sat on a branch near it, and the cat sat next to the hawk.

"I found no way through the fog," said Finn.

"Nor will you," said the harp. "Now listen to what we have learned, we three. It is a magic fog, sowed by a hundred

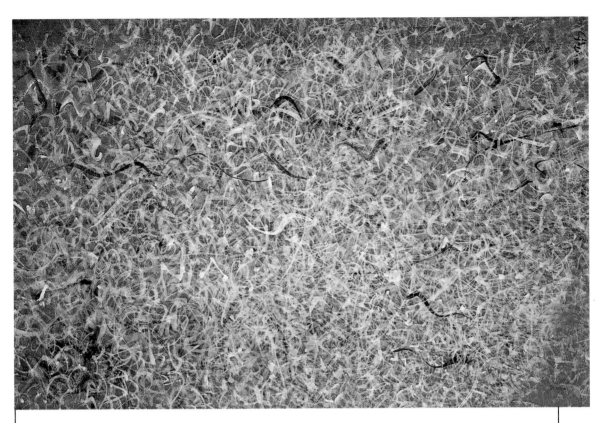

"It is a magic fog,
sowed by a hundred mist crones . . . "

mist crones, flying in formation. They are the daughters of Drabne, whom you thwarted thrice and damaged severely, and they have vowed your destruction."

"But why the fog?"

"To hide McMorna from you and prevent your challenge. And, it is said, Goll will stay hidden until this coven, and the assorted demons they have espoused, cook up a tactic that will assure your defeat."

"Things don't seem to be going so well," said Finn.

"Not well at all, my boy. You need some influence in high

places too, or you'll never get to lead the Fianna. All you'll be leading is your own funeral procession."

"What shall I do?"

"Seek the help of a god."

"I don't know any who'll help me. In fact, I don't know any at all."

"Try a goddess, then. Perhaps you'll do better in that direction."

"What goddess?"

"Amara, Queen of the Harvest. You may have pleased her without knowing it. She has always loathed Drabne in all her guises, and must have rejoiced in her defeat."

"Really? You think she might help me?"

"It's worth a try. You have nothing to lose."

"Come then," said Finn. "We'll look for Amara."

He found her under an oak tree, picking acorns. It was the largest oak in Eire, perhaps in the world. Unimaginably old, with a huge bole, massive limbs, and deep-ridged bark. It was called the Druid Oak, and was Amara's favorite place.

She was so tall she could stand under the tree and put fallen birds back into the nest merely by reaching her arm. Clad in green she was; her hair hung thick and yellow as sheaves of wheat. As Finn approached her he became aware of the fragrance arising from her bare shoulders; she smelled of sunshine and crushed grass. Her beauty robbed Finn of his sense; he could hardly speak.

"Do you seek me, lad?" she called.

"I seek you, O Queen of the Harvest. I seek your favor."

"Speak."

"I go in search of my enemy, Goll McMorna, and my cause is just. But he is being aided by witches and demons and the devil knows who, and I need help in high places."

"Mine, you mean."

"If you please."

"I must tell you this: Any favor I show you will be more than offset by the wrath of Vilemurk, the Foul-weather Fiend, Blighter of Crops, and my age-old enemy. Any friend of mine is a foe of his, and his rage is terrible."

"Your favor, I trow, is worth his wrath."

"One more thing. You should understand that a god's favor can damage a weak man beyond repair—that it can twist him and blast him until it seems like a curse."

"Ah, Lady, I am accustomed to risk. And I have already been blessed or cursed by the sight of your beauty. I will take all you have to give, if you do the giving."

"You will obey me in all things?"

"I will."

"Stand there, then, and accept what comes."

She stretched her arms high. Her tall radiance blotted the weak sunlight. The afternoon was stunned by her beauty. The brook stopped chattering, and the wind held its breath. The rough meadow grass stiffened. The Druid Oak stretched huge arms toward her, then tore itself out of the ground and hobbled toward her on its twisted roots. The birds, shaken from their nests, chided as they came. Finn would have fled the tree, but Amara pushed him into the thick of its brush. He tried to lunge away but could not break loose; he was tangled in a vine. Amara laughed and wound another coil of vine about him, binding him fast.

"Do not struggle, foolish one," said Amara. "Let him take you into his oaken embrace. Do you not know him? He is the Sacred Oak, broken shadow of the eldest god, who has taken root in this place and drinks its living waters, and grows huge and lusty, putting out blossoms, dropping acorns. He is a god, a rough, wooden, shade-giving god. He is the oak of your clan, Finn, vined by mistletoe, that magic loop. Yield . . . yield . . .

it is a father's embrace. He is of your father too, this oak; his long taproot drinks of dead kings."

Finn stopped struggling. In the music of her voice, he gave himself to the idea of the oak. A green drowse fell upon him, and he slept.

When he awoke he was sitting in the shade of the Druid Oak, which had rooted itself again. Dusk had fallen, and a cold wind blew. Amara spoke to him:

"You have taken a step toward understanding. Now do this: Strip yourself naked despite the cold, or rather because of the cold, so that you will be frozen away from your own self, so that your blood will slow and a silence come upon you, and a stillness upon your fancy, and you will invent nothing and claim nothing, but give yourself to perfect attention. After three days we will come together, and I shall hear what you have learned."

And so it was done. Finn sank into the ground past the roots of grass and flowers and the gnarled clutch of the oak to a warm place where waters are born out of underground steam. After three days he thawed, and clawed his way up again into light, disturbing moles.

Amara was waiting for him under the oak tree. "Did you dwell in that darkness?" she said.

"Yes."

"In the silence?"

"I did."

"Were you cold?"

"I was."

"Did the darkness and the silence and the cold help you to perfect attention?"

"They did."

"Did light come to you in the darkness?"

"The only light came from a kind of dream that happened outside my head, not inside. A bright picture floated before me

"Do you seek me, lad?"
she called.

in the darkness. I saw low burned hills and a flash of sea. And things tearing the earth—pecking metal lizards all over, eating every inch of space, swarming on the beaches, filling the air with a brown oily smell, coming out of the earth to eat the living green. I felt my heart being devoured, Amara, as I watched the metal lizards eating the trees and pecking at the sand and drinking the margins of the sea. What were they? What did I see?"

"Mineral devils."

"And what are they?"

"They belong to the kingdom of Vilemurk. As Frost Demon and Lord of Misrule, he is King of the Mineral Devils. But you saw more in your vision. What else did you see?"

"It was too horrible. I cannot bear to remember."

"You are my warrior. You must look horror in the face, and not flinch. Tell me what you saw."

"The mineral devils making a mineral masterpiece—a great egg that breaks into fire when it is laid by mineral birds. And the birds were in the air, dropping their eggs of fire, smashing cities, igniting the dust, fusing bones and beams, roasting the cattle in their fields and the fish in the lake." His face was wet with tears. "What was it, Amara, what did I see?"

"You saw man himself as mineral devil. In your vision of time to come, he has turned away from the living gods and worships himself as mineral devil. Vilemurk triumphs, Drabne prevails. My crops are dead and I am dead. Man has turned his trees to spikes, his grass to barbs, and his path is stone."

"Will this come to pass? Must it be?"

"There is no 'must' in human affairs, O boy-who-would-be-a-man. That is a Vilemurk idea. The mineral devils want man to believe that his future can be read in the cold and mathematical stars. And so man loses hope, loses joy, and abandons himself to the devil-gods of industry, artifice, anthill order. He trades his warm living body for a cold idea. Sells himself to the smith

"Man has turned his trees to spikes,
his grass to barbs,
and his path is stone."

demons, to the Vilemurk vision, the Drabne design. Chains himself to anvil and stokes the forge fires until he drops from exhaustion or is flogged to death."

"Every word you speak, Amara, whets my appetite for battle. . . . Speaking of smiths, though, I wish I had a better blade." He drew his sword and looked at it ruefully. "This is well enough, but I wish I had my father's blue sword. It was taken from him when he was killed. Some McMorna has it now."

Amara said: "You will use no sword when you fight Goll McMorna."

"No sword?" cried Finn. "Why not?"

"They are made of metal, and metal belongs to Vilemurk."

"This sword belongs to me."

"Its metal belongs to Vilemurk and will not serve you. Goll McMorna is Vilemurk's man. Right now he is in the smithy, being armed by mineral devils. They are dressing him in metal. When he faces you he will wear brass armor and carry an iron sword."

"How will I be armed?"

"With a hawthorn stick and a bag of seed. You will wear no armor, but a light woolen tunic, dyed green. No iron hat, but a crown of leaves. You will wield a hawthorn stick. At your belt will hang a bag of seed."

"And Goll will be wearing—what again?"

"Breastplate and greaves of bright brass. He will carry a spear for throwing, and a huge two-handed sword for close work—and a battle-ax slung."

"A stick against a sword?" said Finn. "Goll is a fearsome warrior in his own right, you know, even without this inequality of arms. What chance will I have?"

"The chance I give you. Which means the chance you give yourself."

"I don't understand."

"Your weapons will do for you only what you do for them. You must make them extensions of yourself. Infuse them with your own virtue. They will respond to your courage; smite with your strength, take their edge from your fineness."

"A stick against a sword . . . wood against iron . . ."

"Wood is alive. Iron is wood, long dead. The devils are dead gods."

"Help me to understand."

"You have seen a horrible vision of man as mineral devil, consuming the earth with mineral fire. But that vision will begin to come true only when the weapons that men wield are stronger than man himself. On that day he begins to lose both strength and honor, and gives himself to the mineral devil. Do you understand?"

"I'm trying to."

"You have come to me, Amara, Goddess of Growing Things. You are son of the oak, harvest prince, my green hero. You cannot bear metal. You must use the living tools I give you."

"Shall I cut my stick from that hawthorn tree?"

"I'll break it off. No blade must touch it."

"And the bag of seed?"

"I'll teach you its use."

Amara taught Finn how to use the seeds. They were acorns of the Druid Oak. Now, the roots of an oak tree go very deep. They sink themselves into the soil as far as they can, and grapple the earth hungrily. The bigger the tree, the longer its roots. And this Druid Oak was the biggest tree in all Eire, and perhaps in all the world.

"Keep the seeds in your pouch," Amara said. "And keep the pouch at your belt. The seeds will hunger to sink themselves into the earth and put out roots, so that you will be given an enormous family pull toward earth. Each time you touch the earth you will feel new strength coursing through your body, the incredible, stubborn, sappy strength of living things—the green strength, the magical plant strength which can push a tiny flower through a floor of stone, the flower we call saxifrage. So imagine what power it gives to the oak and the seeds of the oak.

". . . this Druid Oak was the biggest tree
in all Eire, and perhaps
in all the world."

And that power, Finn, will flow through you when you touch
the earth. With sword and battle-ax Goll will try to beat down
your guard and beat you to earth. But if he does, you will drink
of its strength and arise renewed."

"And the seeds stay always in my pouch?" said Finn. "And
the pouch at my belt?"

"Only if you know you face death the next instant may
you take a seed from the pouch. Then take only one, and cast it
upon the earth. But remember—only if you face death. If you

do it before that time you will have scattered your strength and must fall under the blows of your enemy."

"I shall remember," said Finn.

"Go now. I shall watch over you. I—Amara, Lady of the Grove, Bride of the Oak, Queen of the Harvest, Goddess of Growing Things. Take of my strength. Drink of my bounty. Strike a blow for the quick, the living, the warm-blooded. Blessings of the seed be upon you, of the root and the blossom. Murmurous blessing of the leaves. Be of good cheer, have no fear, strike with joy. The grace of all natural strokes be with you—from tiger paw to leaf fall. Bless you, Finn, bless you. Your victory is ours."

She knelt and took him into her meadow-sweet embrace, kissed him upon the lips, leaving him reeling with happiness, and unafraid.

All of Eire had come to see the battle, it seemed. Upon the great plain of Meath before the walls of Tara were assembled the bravest and fairest in all the land. The fog had blown away. A slant sun fell; the air was blue and smoky. Tents and pavilions flashed upon the plain, striped blue and crimson. Struck into the ground stood a forest of pennants—the colors of the warrior chief, colors of the fighting clans. The tents of the Fianna were green and gold; they sat in one cluster. The High King sat on the royal stone—three slabs of rock forming a natural throne—on a hill overlooking the plain. He sat there, his gold crown on his head, gold staff in his hand. His royal guard surrounded him. Standing there too, leaning on their spears, were the twelve brothers of Goll McMorna, underchiefs of the Fianna. The ladies of the court stood with their men. They wore gowns of silk and wreaths of flowers in their hair. They were tall and free limbed and easy laughing. They often accompanied their men into battle, and were sometimes feared more than the men themselves.

There were others there too—a dreadful legion whom no one saw. They had the power of keeping themselves invisible to mortal eyes until they chose to appear. These were Drabne's daughters and Vilemurk's cohorts, summoned there to help Goll, if needed. Mist crones and frost demons, the Master of Winds, and Vilemurk himself, of course. He was too important for complete invisibility, though; all you could see of him was the edge of his beard, like a fleecy cloud.

The king raised his staff. Trumpets cried. Goll McMorna entered the field, riding a huge black horse. Lances of sunlight shivered on his breastplate of brass and his brass greaves. He carried a long spear for throwing, a great two-handed sword for closer work, and a battle-ax slung. A mighty shout arose when he appeared. He stood in his stirrups and shook his spear. The shouting doubled and redoubled until the glade rang with the voices of the fighting men of Eire. The Fianna added its keening eagle war cry, and each clan answered with its own battle shout.

Then Finn came into the field. There was a great collective sighing gasp of wonder and disappointment. He didn't seem like he was coming to fight at all. Where Goll was all massive heaviness and brassy strength, Finn—clad in green, unmounted, walking across the field—seemed to have the lightness of the meadow grass itself, which was barely disturbed as he walked. Light footed he came. He wore no armor, only his woolen tunic, dyed green. On his head was a crown of oak leaves. All he bore in the way of arms was a hawthorn stick and a wicker shield. At his belt was a leather bag.

The king raised his staff again. The trumpets sounded a challenge. Finn stood on the grass, facing Goll, and called:

"I, Finn McCool, son of Cuhal, grandson of the oak, wearer of Amara's green, accuse you, Goll, son of Morna, of my father's murder and wrongful claim to the chieftainship of the Fianna. I challenge you to mortal combat."

Goll sat on his horse like a brass statue. His voice rang like brass as he answered:

"I, Goll McMorna, scourge of the Clan Cuhal, chief of the Fianna, wearing tomorrow's bright metal, give the lie to all you say. I accuse you of conduct unbecoming a member of the Fianna. I accuse you of salmon poaching, witch baiting, cat theft, hawk theft, and of foul tampering with the sacred Druid feast. I accept your challenge, and shall prove your guilt upon your body."

The king raised his staff again; the trumpets sounded a third time. The fight began.

Goll set his lance, crouched in his saddle, and spurred his horse into a thundering gallop. Finn stood there, waiting. The crowd gasped, seeing the slender youth hold his ground before the huge horse hurtling toward him. At the very last second Finn seemed to sway away without moving his feet. Goll's lance whistled past his shoulder; the great horse rushed past, just grazing his tunic, and hurtled to the other side of the field before Goll could rein him up.

Finn stood there, waiting, a smile on his face. He still had not moved his feet. Again Goll charged. Again Finn swayed like a river reed touched by a breeze. Again the stallion's shoulder grazed his tunic as it stormed past. And Finn stood there, unhurt, still smiling.

Now Goll changed tactics. He made the horse walk slowly, like a cat stalking a bird, over the field toward Finn. Goll poised himself in the saddle, sword held high. Finn left his place then and circled very slowly, crouching slightly, holding his wicker shield in one hand and the hawthorn stick in the other. Goll walked his horse in tightening circles around Finn until he towered over the boy—then raised his sword and brought it crashing down. The crowd shouted at this terrific blow, expecting to see the heavy blade split Finn vertically, like a cook slicing a celery stalk.

Finn held up his wicker shield slantwise so that the sword fell upon it, but glancingly, and was deflected. The blow was so powerful that Goll almost fell from his saddle, but he recovered quickly, raised his sword again, and struck another blow, which, this time, Finn deflected with a whisk of his stick. Finn's blow was so swift it was almost invisible, slashing Goll across the wrist at the moment of downstroke, so that the huge blade was again made to swerve, but this time with terrible effect.

The edge of the blade hit Goll's horse full upon the chest. The black stallion whinnied in agony and threw itself backward, flinging Goll clear, then rolling over the grass in his death throes. But the man was such a superb warrior that he did not allow this fall to unbalance him, but twisted in the air and landed crouching on his feet. Goll rushed toward Finn, slashing with his sword. Finn circled slowly, weaving shield and stick, deflecting the heavy blows. But Goll was enraged by the death of his horse. He was swept with battle fury, fired with a savage strength such as he had never known. He battered at Finn with his heavy sword until, finally, the blade sheared through the wicker shield—which turned it enough so that the flat of the blade fell upon Finn's shoulder. But it was a paralyzing blow. Finn felt his arm and shoulder go numb. Before he could recover, Goll had cut at him with a vicious backhanded stroke, slashing his right arm, and he could barely hold the hawthorn stick.

He leaped aside to avoid a third blow, but was so weakened by the loss of blood he fell to earth. Finn immediately felt a giant sappy strength flowing through him, stanching his blood, filling him with an ecstasy of vigor. An amazed Goll saw the youth, beaten to earth a second before, spring up and face him again, smiling.

Now Finn moved so lightly that to strike him was like attacking a butterfly with a club. He floated away from Goll's

*"I, Goll McMorna, . . . wearing tomorrow's
bright metal, give the lie
to all you say."*

blows, then slid in again jabbing with his pointed stick, stinging like a hornet. Again and again he touched Goll on the parts of his body not covered by brass—his arms, his legs above the greaves, his face beneath the helmet.

The crowd, wondering, saw the mighty Goll stop and stand, bewildered, like a man attacked in the glade by a swarm of hornets. They saw him wipe the blood from his face and paw at Finn with his sword. But the boy was all about him, stabbing, dancing in and out so fast the eye could not follow, and Goll could not touch him with his blade.

Now Vilemurk took a hand. He whistled up a hailstorm— a small one—which fell on the field from a cloudless sky, and spat ice at Finn as he stalked toward the confused Goll. And Finn, stepping across the field, ready for a final attack, full of confidence and cold joy, suddenly felt his feet slipping . . . slipping. He shuffled desperately, trying to keep his balance—for Goll had recovered and was coming toward him.

Then he lost sight of Goll completely. He saw nothing. He was blinded by a moist grayness that pressed upon him, snuffing the sun, blotting his sight. The crowd lost sight of him and could not understand. Where he stood was a column of fog. What had happened was that the mist crones, signaled by Vilemurk, had flown down invisibly to join the hailstorm and cast their fog upon Finn, fitting it as closely as a garment.

Goll, standing on the sunny field, saw the misty shape of his foe, stumbling and groping, and was able to approach without any danger to himself. He walked up to the column of mist and began to slash it with his sword, slashing again and again, leaving the mist in tatters.

The brothers of Goll raised their eagle cry as they saw Finn stagger out of the fog, bleeding from a hundred wounds. They saw him sway, and sink to earth. But Vilemurk understood now that Finn was renewing himself every time he touched the earth, and he would not let that happen again. He whistled a third time. The Master of Winds shook a small tornado out of his cloak—a black funneling spout of wind. It whirled down on Finn, seized him, whirled him on the grass, bleeding as he was, then lifted him into the air and held him aloft so that he could not touch the earth.

Finn hung in the air, almost dead. Goll had thrown off his helmet. He walked slowly to where Finn floated, shoulder high,

*The Master of Winds shook a small
tornado out of his cloak—a
black funneling spout of wind.*

drawing his dagger as he went. Goll's hair was red as blood. His face was greenish white, cheese colored, dewed with sweat, twitching with delight. He wound his left hand into Finn's black hair and drew back his head, stretching his neck. Then he raised his knife.

Finn's thoughts were dim as his life bled away. He felt the hand of his enemy on his head, but in his dimness the heavy hand felt like a caress. A thought floated free:

"Time to cast the seed, for, surely, I'll never be any closer to death than this."

His fingers twitched at his belt, but he had lost too much strength. He could not untie the leather pouch and cast the seed. He saw Goll's knife glittering above his head.

Then, in the hills, Amara laughed.

Goll was taking his time, raising the knife high, admiring how it flashed in the sun, knowing the crowd was hypnotized by the flashing blade too, and that they were watching him, Goll, standing triumphant over his fallen foe. And as the knife glittered, Amara laughed. Finn, with his last failing sense, heard her laugh. And Goll heard her laugh. He stood there, arm high, transfixed by the wild music of her laughter. All the vast crowd heard that laughter.

No one knew what it was; no one had heard anything like it. There was something of the hawk's cry in her laughter, of lark-thronging dawns. Of the tumbling of waters. Of mare trumpeting, answering stallions on the hill. In her laughter was gaudy summer and the million-voiced murmur of grass, and the hush of a pumpkin moon.

The dimming spark of Finn's life flickered in the gust of that laughter, and flared briefly. His fingers twitched again at the mouth of the pouch and worked it open. He plucked an acorn from the bag and let it drop to earth—just as Goll recovered from his hesitation and slashed downward at Finn's throat.

The seed was quicker. An oak sapling sprouted with magic speed, striking Goll's arm, knocking the dagger aside. A hedge of saplings sprang between Finn and Goll, shutting Goll off from his prey, forcing them further and further apart—one sapling then another springing from the ground, locking their branches, twining their twigs, making a brambly hedge for Goll—a leafy cell. He struggled and plunged but could not free himself. Vines caught his arms and legs. He was a prisoner of growth.

Vilemurk saw what was happening. He gestured to the

Master of Winds, who immediately flung a sharp-edged gale to scythe down the hedge. But the downdraft of the gale hit Finn and pressed him to earth. As soon as he touched earth his wounds closed; his mind cleared. A sappy green strength coursed through him, and he sprang to his feet, bright as morning.

The gale scythed down the saplings. The hedge was falling. Goll was struggling free. Finn picked up his hawthorn stick and let himself be taken by the gale. He went flying across the field like a leaf—going with enormous speed, holding the pointed stick. And when he hit Goll he had all the force of the gale behind him—that force which has been known to drive a splinter of wood through a stone wall. The hawthorn stick went through the brass breastplate like a needle through cloth and came out the other side. Goll fell heavily, gaffed like a trout.

Finn stood over him, hair ruffled by the wind, eyes glowing. He raised his hawthorn stick on high and lifted his voice in the great victory cry of the Fianna. The Fianna called back. He was their chief now.

The Clan McMorna howled their grief. The daughters of Drabne screeched in rage as they flew off. Vilemurk made no sound; he departed invisibly, planning vengeance. He would have to wait, he knew, but he could do that. Foul-weather fiends are very patient.

The hawk screamed with joy. The cat cried murder and amour.

Finn lifted his face toward the sky. He was not smiling. His face was not that of a boy, but of a man who has killed an enemy who was trying to kill him.

Amara laughed again from the hills.

Acknowledgments

Cover, DRABNE OF DOLE *(1989) by Hrana Janto, pencil, watercolor, pastel, and acrylic (10"*
× 13")
   Courtesy of the artist

Opposite page 1, *Detail from* THE WITCH *by Sir John Gilbert (1817–97), oil on canvas*
   Courtesy of the Guildhall Art Gallery, London
      Photo: Bridgeman/Art Resource, NY

Page 3, THE ARTIST'S SON *by Peter Paul Rubens (1577–1640), chalk on paper*
   Courtesy of the Albertina Museum, Vienna
      Photo: Marburg/Art Resource, NY

Page 6, NUMBER 7, 1952 *by Jackson Pollock (1912–56), pen and ink on paper*
      Photo: Art Resource, NY

Page 11, PAN *by Frederick William MacMonnies (1863–1937), bronze*
   Courtesy of Christie's, NY

Page 14, *Detail from* EVE *by Lucas Cranach, the Elder (1472–1553), oil on canvas*
   Courtesy of the Museum of Art, Antwerp
      Photo: Giraudon/Art Resource, NY

Page 16, SMALL BACCHANALIA *by Pablo Picasso (1881–1973), linoleum cut (block printed in*
black, brown, and beige; Arches paper) Edition: 50 (image 8 5/8" × 10 3/8")
   Courtesy of the Metropolitan Museum of Art, Mr. and Mrs. Charles Kramer
   Collection, Gift of Mr. and Mrs. Charles Kramer, 1979 (1979.620.45)

Page 18, PELICAN *by John James Audubon (1785–1851), print*
   Courtesy of the New York Public Library
      Photo: Scala/Art Resource, NY

Page 22, AMELIA PALMER *by Charles Ingham Cromwell (1796–1863), oil on canvas (67 7/8" × 53 1/4")*
 Courtesy of the Metropolitan Museum of Art, Gift of Courtlandt Palmer, 1950 (50.220.1)

Page 25, THE ARTIST'S MOTHER *by Albrecht Dürer (1471–1528), pen and ink and chalk on paper*
 Photo: Marburg/Art Resource, NY

Page 28, UNTITLED *(1989) by Jerry Burchfield, cibachrome monoprints*
 Courtesy of the artist and Merging One Gallery, Santa Monica

Page 31, NARCISSUS *by Michelangelo Merisi da Caravaggio (1573–1610), oil on canvas*
 Courtesy of the National Gallery, Rome
 Photo: Scala/Art Resource, NY

Page 35, *Detail from* THE PLEASURE OF FISHES *(late 13th century), Chinese hand scroll, Chou Tung Ching, ink and colors on paper (12 1/8" × 233 3/4")*
 Courtesy of the Metropolitan Musuem of Art, Fletcher Fund, 1947 (47.18.30)
 Photo: Bob Hanson

Page 40, RED VARIATION XIV-A (CURRENT) *(1989) by Michael Rubin, acrylic on canvas (46" × 46")*
 Courtesy of the artist and Philip Samuels Fine Art, St. Louis

Page 43, *Detail from* LE PETIT BRÉVIAIRE DE JEANNE D'EVREUX, *2nd vol., fol. 53v. (14th century), illuminated manuscript*
 Courtesy of the Musée Condé, Chantilly
 Photo: Giraudon/Art Resource, NY

Page 46, FALCON *by Antonio Pisanello (ca. 1395–1455), pen and ink on paper*
 Courtesy of the Louvre, Paris
 Photo: Giraudon/Art Resource, NY

Page 49, *Detail from* THE HUNT OF THE UNICORN *(ca. 1500), Franco-Flemish tapestry; silk, wool, silver, and silver-gilt threads (12' 1" × 10' 4")*
 Courtesy of the Metropolitan Museum of Art, gift of John D. Rockefeller, Jr., Cloisters Collection, 1937 (37.80.1)

Page 52, ORION IN WINTER *by Charles Burchfield (1893–1967), oil on canvas*
 Courtesy of the Thyssen-Bornemisza Collection
 Photo: Art Resource, NY

Page 54, FEMALE STATUETTE *(ca. 1950–1550 B.C.), cypriot terra cotta, black-slip ware*
 Courtesy of the Metropolitan Museum of Art, Cesnola Collection, purchased by subscription 1874–76 (74.51.1544)

Page 57, WATER OF THE FLOWERY MILL *by Arshile Gorky (1905–48), oil on canvas, (42 3/4" × 48 3/4")*
 Courtesy of the Metropolitan Museum of Art, George A. Hearn Fund, 1956 (56.205.1)

Page 60, *Tile (late 18th century) tin-glazed earthenware, transfer-printed and green decoration*
 Courtesy of the Cooper-Hewitt Museum, NY

Page 62, YOUNG MAN WITH A CROWN OF VINES *(1962) by Pablo Picasso, linoleum cut (block printed in black, dark brown, light brown, and beige; Arches paper) (image 13 7/8" × 10 5/8")*
 Courtesy of the Metropolitan Museum of Art, Mr. and Mrs. Charles Kramer Collection, Gift of Mr. and Mrs. Charles Kramer, 1979 (1979.620.76)

Page 65, WORLD DUST *by Mark Tobey (1890–1976), gouache, ink on Japanese paper (37" × 25")*
Courtesy of the Metropolitan Museum of Art, Arthur Hoppock Hearn Fund, 1958 (58.25)

Page 69, CERES *(ca. 1505) by Antoine Dufour, detail from Vie des femmes célèbres, illuminated manuscript*
Courtesy of the Musée Dobrée, Nantes
Photo: Giraudon/Art Resource, NY

Page 71, THE INVISIBLES *by Yves Tanguy (1900–1955), oil on canvas*
Courtesy of the Tate Gallery, London
Photo: Tate Gallery/Art Resource, NY

Page 74, THE BODMER OAK, FONTAINEBLEU FOREST *by Claude Oscar Monet (1840–1926), oil on canvas (37 7/8" × 50 7/8")*
Courtesy of the Metropolitan Museum of Art, Gift of Sam Salz and Bequest of Julia W. Emmonds, by exchange, 1964 (64.210)
Photo: Malcolm Varon

Page 79, *English helmet (1590) made for George Clifford, third earl of Cumberland, K.G., steel and gilt*
Courtesy of the Metropolitan Museum of Art, Munsey Fund, 1932 (32.130.6a-y)

Page 81, UNTITLED (PH-114) *by Clyfford Still (1904–80), oil on canvas (91 3/4" × 70 3/4")*
Courtesy of the Metropolitan Museum of Art, Gift of Mrs. Clyfford Still, 1986 (1986.441.3)
Photo: Lynton Gardiner

DATE DUE

MAR 14 1992			
AUG 17 1992			
JUN 12 1993			
APR 30 1994			
OCT 19 1995			
JAN 20 1997			
JY 03 '98			
OC 29 '98			
MY 27 '99			
JAN 13 2008			
APR 26 2013			
SEP 05 2013			

DEMCO 38-297